The

REAL
MATRIX

MICHAEL EVANS

authorHOUSE®

AuthorHouse™
1663 Liberty Drive
Bloomington, IN 47403
www.authorhouse.com
Phone: 1 (800) 839-8640

© *2015 Michael Evans. All rights reserved.*

No part of this book may be reproduced, stored in a retrieval system, or transmitted by any means without the written permission of the author.

Published by AuthorHouse   11/17/2015

ISBN: 978-1-5049-5478-5 (sc)
ISBN: 978-1-5049-5476-1 (hc)
ISBN: 978-1-5049-5477-8 (e)

Library of Congress Control Number: 2015916588

Print information available on the last page.

Any people depicted in stock imagery provided by Thinkstock are models, and such images are being used for illustrative purposes only. Certain stock imagery © Thinkstock.

This book is printed on acid-free paper.

Because of the dynamic nature of the Internet, any web addresses or links contained in this book may have changed since publication and may no longer be valid. The views expressed in this work are solely those of the author and do not necessarily reflect the views of the publisher, and the publisher hereby disclaims any responsibility for them.

DEDICATION

This book is dedicated to Amy, Jocelyn, Michael and Matthew. After a million lifetimes of searching, we found each other here and now. For the record, you were all worth the wait. The one thing I have always wanted to give you is in this book; my heart.

To my mother and my brothers; every left and every right has led us to where we are today; a far cry from where we were 40 years ago. I'm proud to call you my family.

To Alexa; if you find yourself getting lost in life, pay attention to your heart; the place where I will be when you need me, now and forever.

Michael Evans

To the reader; "The whole theory of the universe is directed unerringly to one individual -namely to you." -Walt Whitman

Welcome to the afternoon of your life.

-Michael

Contents

Dedication v

Foreword ix

Introduction xvii

Chapter 1 1
The Real Matrix

Chapter 2 19
How do we get out of the Matrix?

Chapter 3 29
The Law of Attraction and the Dream of Your Life

Chapter 4 37
There's Nothing to Worry About

Chapter 5 51
Getting Off of Autopilot

Chapter 6 59
The Real Butterfly Effect

Chapter 7 67
The Death of Your Old Self

FOREWORD

Something really interesting is happening in the world right now. Ok, it's been happening for quite some time, thousands of years really, but it's becoming much more apparent lately. More and more people are waking up. You've probably read or heard somewhere that this is the time of the "Great Awakening", and you may have wondered what the hell that really means. Waking up from *what*, exactly?

We're waking up to the knowledge of who we really are. We're waking up from the idea that this physical reality is actually real and all there is, and coming into

Michael Evans

the conscious realization that what we're experiencing in our daylight hours is actually the dream. We're waking up from powerlessness, the self-imposed prison we've been uncomfortably and desperately squeezing ourselves into, and we're throwing open the doors, walking out into the sun and squishing our toes in the grass. We're remembering that we're infinitely powerful, creative beings who are here not to suffer and produce and pay our dues or prove ourselves worthy, but to create and play and experience and enjoy. We're waking up to the inherent knowledge, that voice that's been there all along, sometimes whispering, now often shouting at us that this is not a rehearsal – some trial by fire where we're supposed to prove our mettle while looking forward to the real deal. *This* is the real deal. The good stuff isn't coming to us after we die (providing we've suffered enough

The Real Matrix

and some outside authority judges us to be deserving of it), it's here right now.

You actually do create your own reality. In fact, you are your reality. You are the Universe. You are the divine. You are everything that is, has been and will be. Yeah, I know. That's some scary stuff. I mean, if you're actually that powerful, then why isn't your world filled with sunshine and rainbows? Well, it is, actually. But it's probably also filled with a lot of other crap that isn't so happy and shiny. But that isn't because it *can't* be, it's simply because a world that has been asleep did an incredibly good job convincing you to suppress and forget your power.

When you came to this planet, you didn't speak the language. You couldn't walk or use your body in any meaningful way. You couldn't even see or hear

Michael Evans

very well, and were totally dependent on those already here – the natives – for your survival. You really had no choice but to copy them. So, you did as they did, said what they said, and believed what they believed. If they told you that your survival depended on you working really hard and being largely unhappy, then you accepted that, even if it contradicted your own customs and knowledge and made no sense to you. You may have had a sense of remembering that this wasn't the only way to do things, and that suffering wasn't at all necessary and certainly not the best way to produce success, that in fact, you were supposed to enjoy yourself here, but you were willing to submit to the "wisdom" of the natives. After all, they were bigger than you and had managed to survive for years in this environment without dying. They had to know something, right?

The Real Matrix

So, you took on their customs; you conformed; you did your best to be content with what you were told to be content with (even if you actually weren't). Only, it didn't work. That voice inside you grew louder: "You're supposed to be happy. You're supposed to enjoy this. It's supposed to easy. There's so much more to this dream than you've been told." And that voice has led you here, wherever "here" is for you – to this exact moment in your life, to this book.

The first time I met Michael Evans, he sent me an article he'd written. Now, I get a lot of people sending me their work, asking me to share it with my audience. Most of it languishes unread in my inbox, because I simply don't have the time to cope with the sheer volume. Michael didn't ask me for anything; he only added a note that he thought I might find

Michael Evans

what he'd written to be interesting. His mail got my attention by pretty much jumping out at me in my inbox, and I was compelled to click on the link and not only read it, but share it on all my social media. I then looked him up and found out he was an ex-police officer, writing articles about energy and personal development and who we really are. I had no idea what kind of manifestation was in the works here; I only knew it was going to be really, really awesome.

When we subsequently spoke on the phone a few months later, I was immediately struck by his immense energy. As someone who has dedicated her life to assisting others with their awakening and helping to make the ride a bit smoother, I recognized a kindred spirit in Michael. This was a man who had stepped

The Real Matrix

firmly into his power. This was someone who "got" it. This was someone who had woken up.

I learned that Michael owns a security agency, protecting people from kidnapping. This remarkable man enters into this dark world of violence and pain and brings his incredible light to it. He employs and coaches soldiers who come back from war on how to overcome depression. He helps abused women escape their nightmare situations and then counsels them to become more empowered and finally build lives of strength and joy.

When he asked me if I'd like to write the foreword to his new book, I was incredibly honored. When I had the pleasure of reading the manuscript a couple of weeks later, that feeling doubled. Michael is a beautiful story teller and skillfully weaves analogies that make

Michael Evans

incredibly complex issues as simple as child's play. There is a tremendous amount of energy in his words (as there is in him), and I cannot imagine anyone reading this book and not being changed by the experience. It's time to wake up, and if you're reading this book, you've already begun. Your world is about to change in the most awesome way and nothing will ever be the same again. Are you ready?

Melody Fletcher

Author of "Deliberate Receiving: Finally the Universe makes some freaking sense!"

INTRODUCTION

As I contemplated exactly what to write as an introduction to this book, I realized that, in writing the answers to the following interview for the book's press release, I had already written an introduction. And so, I present, The Real Matrix.

Interview for Press Release

1. What inspired your journey into spiritualism?

Spiritualism was something that I gravitated toward about 15 years ago. After about 5 years of studying psychology, in particular the works of Carl Jung, whose

Michael Evans

philosophy was, when you look inside of yourself, you awaken, but when you look outside of yourself, you dream – I began to look at the ancient wisdom of the Toltecs. The first time I read the Mastery of Love, I was not only in awe of what I was reading, I was relieved. I was relieved to hear that all of the conclusions I was drawing as a result of my studying teachers like Emerson and more recently, Wayne Dyer, were in line with ancient masters of themselves – the Toltecs. Toltecs were known as "Artists of the Spirit" and they understood what most people have forgotten today; that we are dreaming all of the time and creating our realities.

2. **What saved you from your brush with suicide? Was it a particular book or lecture?**

It was a decision I made, pretty much, without any knowledge of psychology or spirituality whatsoever. I

The Real Matrix

had never even heard of a self-help book or spirituality when I was 18 years old. I had a near death experience one night when I was driving home from a nightclub with a friend. The event was not something most people have experienced, and it was the beginning of my new life. I was driving home at about 4am on the Long Island Expressway Service Road. The expressway was often closed in the middle of the night for construction (as it was that night) and vehicles were forced to drive on the service road. I was driving at about 60 miles per hour when I approached an intersection with a traffic light. My light was green. As I approached the light, something inside of me said to let go of the accelerator. I even said it out loud in a question to whatever or whoever just told this to me, I said, "Slow down, Mike?" So I let go of the accelerator and at that exact moment, a car speeding through a

Michael Evans

red light crossed my path. The freakiest part of this incident was that the car that would surely have killed me – had I not slowed down – was speeding, but I saw the driver – clear as day – as if he had stopped in front of me. Time actually stopped for a second and I saw every detail of this driver. He was asleep at the wheel and I could describe him today as if it happened this morning. Just then, I had a knowing that I had some work to do here while I'm still alive. In my mind, the old me died that day and the new me was going to do whatever it is that I wanted to do, because I was given a second chance. Picture a movie, whereas the character gets to come back from the dead by the work of some supernatural being. I look at it as, maybe I did die that night. Maybe I was given a second chance and that glitch in the Matrix is what I remember and time did stand still. This incident changed everything. I use

The Real Matrix

the inevitable fact that I will die as a motivator to live 27,000 days, instead of 1 day, 27,000 times.

3. **What inspired you to write The Real Matrix?**

I look around this world and I have a hard time standing by – idly – watching people suffer. People believe they are limited. They believe they were born to learn (other people's knowledge in School), accept labels and limitations given to them by their teachers, parents, friends, enemies and popular magazines. They create a self-image that is so out of line with what they really are, that they need medication, alcohol and self-help books to experience happiness. People confuse the needs of the body with the needs of the mind and that leads to debt, obsessions, over eating, racing thoughts and depression. For example, when the body feels the need for food, we get hungry. We

Michael Evans

eat some food and the body is satisfied. However, the mind has its own agenda… MORE! The mind, based upon memes learned as children, has a point of view — it always needs more. People continue to eat long after they are full, because they are trying to satisfy needs that are not real. They do not separate the needs of the body from the needs of the mind. Allowing a mind to run amuck is like having a computer that outthinks the user and takes control of the user. I want to teach people, especially non-readers what has taken me 20+ years to learn. Hopefully, I will plant the seed to start their new journey.

4. **A branch of philosophy has long argued that the world is actually more likely to be artificial intelligences trapped in a fake universe than organic minds in a "real" one. Is the purpose**

of The Real Matrix - to bring this thinking into the mainstream?

The point that I want to make is that nothing happens until something moves. So much of a person's suffering is a result in lies that the person believes about themselves. In order to believe a lie, something that is not happening in the present moment, that person must be dreaming. The relevance of the title of this book is to describe the dream with symbols. Since humans have already mastered the use of symbols with their language – they dream using that language. Humans use symbols to label things, including themselves with the words, "I am." These "I'm" statements are lies we believe about ourselves and they only exist in what I call the matrix; the virtual reality that we create in our minds.

Michael Evans

5. **What differentiates Michael Evans from Wayne Dyer, Eckhart Tolle and others in the New Thought Movement? How are you expanding on ideas presented in "The Secret", "The Power of Now" and similar self-help books? What new messages and ideas are you introducing?**

Wayne Dyer, Eckhart Tolle, Ralph Waldo Emerson, Deepak Chopra and many others are teachers. I've studied and lived these and other teachings for many years. The teachings have led to a mastery of my own life by the understanding that I am creating my reality. The Secret and other works regarding the law of attraction were stepping stones to the reality I have created for myself. What differentiates me from the teachers I have studied is that my story is unique to me. I was looking for the answers to get myself out of

The Real Matrix

hell and when I found them, I made it my life goal to master it and to pass it on to other people in similar positions. Once I understood how life really works, outside of the dream, everything I ever wanted became a reality. Then I began to understand that the things I always wanted - never existed in the first place. I used this knowledge to manifest a business from thin air that has earned me more than $10 million and I can tell you that money is not the key to happiness. My personal story is similar to the stories of many of the potential readers who will use this information as a stepping stone to their new journeys. I'm the living proof that you can have what you ask for. The funny thing is, you will see, once you get it, that simplicity is the ultimate goal and you're closer to it than you know.

Michael Evans

6. **How do you feel about it being called the New Thought Movement? In truth, many of the ideas in New Age are not so new. Take the popular mantra: we are what we think. Ralph Waldo Emerson said, "A man's what he thinks about all day long." The Roman emperor Marcus Aurelius said, "A man's life is what his thoughts make of it." Even the bible says "As a man thinks in his mind, so is he." The bible also says in Genesis that nothing imagined is impossible. The power of concentration and imagination is greater than we realize. What makes these "new" thoughts and why are so many people resistant to them?**

The New Thought Movement is not an accurate description of the lessons taught in this and other

The Real Matrix

self-help books. As I have written in The Real Matrix, the mind dreams, calculates and recalls. Right and wrong comes from your heart by way of intuition. By calling this a new way of thinking, you are suggesting that this is an experiment or a fad. The experiment and the fad are taking place in the mainstream and that is the new thought movement; the movement away from what we really are. As I explain in the autopilot chapter in The Real Matrix, people are acting from subconscious ideas downloaded into their minds when they were children. Those ideas came from our parents, teachers, adults and other people in our lives as children. From those memes, we make an agreement and it becomes part of who we are for the rest of our lives. Just as we create Santa Clause and the Tooth Fairy, we also create other stories that our children believe; stories about them. You're not good at this, you're not

Michael Evans

athletic, you're fat – and they believe it. When they believe these lies, they think about them. When they think about them, they begin to communicate with themselves and others with that lie at the forefront of their thoughts and worse, without the knowledge that their subconscious quickly shoots down opportunities that are presented by auto-implementing the memes that have and continue to create the framework of their dreams. People are resistant to them because they are so pre-occupied with their personal dream. The very people who suffer from emotional pain are the same people who believe the lies I am talking about. When a person who has awakened, tries to explain this information to them, they have a choice; go right back to their Facebook feed or realize the truth. The truth is that only perfection exists. The truth is that they are not the image in the mirror. The truth is that they have been searching for what they lost in the domestication they experienced as children. They have forgotten what they are. It's like trying to explain to the humans that lived thousands of years ago that the moon was not the source of light in the evening. That was always an illusion. The moon was reflecting the light from the sun. The same resistance exists today with people born into this world of lies. We learn lies from the people who teach us how to be humans, when we have always known how to be humans. So, this is not a new way of thinking, this is the original way of thinking. Our lives have been layered with lies, like layers of clothing, one on top of the other and all of it creates the distortion from our true selves to the suffering, guilt machines we have become. The Real Matrix serves to take all of those layers off and get people back to their true selves; their

Michael Evans

naked minds that understand that they are the artist who is creating their reality and their reality can be as beautiful as their thoughts will allow.

7. Are you proposing a no-rules society in "The Real Matrix?"

A no rules society will not work when most of the people in our society are sick; they are sick with a disease called fear. At this point, our medical, pharmaceutical, governmental and educational systems deliver the message that we need all of them to survive. People are considered "normal" when they perform, learn and live within societal rules. The problem is that the people who are living in the matrix are the ones making the rules. Then, what we get is a human who believes they are living as they should and they soon find out that they are not living their life as they

The Real Matrix

would like to. So, this distorted image of themselves is really a projection of a person who is well adjusted to a profoundly sick society.

8. **Beliefs (or memes, as you call them) evolve to fit the times. Marijuana, legal age of consent, slavery, women's rights and gay marriage... is evolution a bad thing?**

Evolution is not a bad thing. However, the dream of the planet leads people to change their point of view to match other people's points of view. Gay marriage is nothing but an idea that people have embraced or pushed against. The theory of evolution is nothing more than a war of ideas. People have created the term marriage, and they have created the term divorce to describe the natural ebb and flow of emotions created between people. It's all a lie. It's not true. People are

Michael Evans

love. The only way to give love is when loves comes out of them, like a pail of water – overflowing. When you believe in lies, religion in particular, you begin to judge what others do, which leads to gossip. Gossip is how people have evolved to communicate. With this gossip (in books, magazines, TV, on the phone, Facebook, etc...) people label things. With these labels are the words gay, lesbian, straight, etc... Then people use these labels to describe their point of view. None of it is real. It never was – including the theory of evolution. It's just a theory, a description of the dream.

9. **What are your thoughts on religion?**

I have been able to see that religion was not meant to be taken literally. Humans use symbols to describe things. I believe that the bible and other religious books were written, using symbols, to describe a story.

The Real Matrix

It's just art and symbols. However, people have taken it literally and personally. They have created their perception of God, which has been perceived very differently among the religions; all that describe life with symbols and stories that are taken literally by the followers of those religions. People kill each other over their defense and promotion of their belief in these stories. I personally do not follow one particular religion. I am open to all religions and stories and attached to none of them.

10. **Do you really believe parents should not interfere in their children's lives? Sure, parents impose their beliefs on children, but as children grow and mature, their free will allows them to formulate their own beliefs based on their own life experiences. Haven't your beliefs**

Michael Evans

changed in time? Aren't we all in a process of enlightenment?

I believe parents should sit back and watch their children live. Parents can learn a lot from a child that has not yet been domesticated. The first few years of a child's life is stress free, judgement free, intuitive living. Young children know love and only love. As parents, we force feed our beliefs that were handed to us when we were children, all of which we didn't choose to believe. I believe parents should teach their children to love from the inside out, or don't, and show them where the self-help books are when they become teenagers. You see, as people get further and further from the truth about whom and what they are, they fall deeper into the matrix. They know that things aren't adding up, but they keep their mouths closed in order to fit into the profoundly sick society they are living in.

11. In a perfect world, how should children be educated?

Children should be taught to think, not to remember battle dates and other people's knowledge. Our education system puts our children into a classification system, based on how well they remember other people's knowledge. I also believe that the current system is setting children up to be workers instead of innovators. Let's face it, we preach family values, then we send children to sit in a classroom for 7 hours a day, only to come home and sit at the kitchen table – buried in homework. What are we teaching them? To take their work home with them; the exact opposite of what we should be teaching them. I know from

Michael Evans

experience that school grades mean nothing in the grand scheme of things. I had the lowest grades in my high school of any student. Once I was inspired to learn something, (for me it was law and criminal justice) I graduated from the degree programs I attended at the very top of my class. I also graduated from 3 of the 5 law enforcement academies I completed with the highest academic grades in the class. I was told by an investigator at one of the first law enforcement agencies I had applied to work for, that "law enforcement is not in your future." Fifteen years of law enforcement, having achieved more than 20 excellent duty awards, proved that theory wrong. I've since written several eBooks in the field of security that continue to sell and help people with their businesses for more than 10 years now. Could you imagine if I had taken my principal's advice to drop out of high school? His

The Real Matrix

advice was based on his belief that I had a learning problem; because I wanted nothing to do with the information they were trying to force-feed me. I didn't agree with a lot of it and that earned me a label, similar to Wayne Dyer's label that he grew up with, "a disturbing element." Many of the readers of The Real Matrix will be people who were mislabeled by a system that measures their ability to remember information. Unfortunately, that information will not be retained and the labels will stick forever if that student agrees with the labels. At the time of this writing, the United States is performing an experiment on its children. That experiment is called "Common Core." Ever since the implementation of this experiment, children are developing psychological symptoms that are just right for the pharmaceutical cure – medication!

Michael Evans

12. Are you opposed to people taking drugs in the treatment of depression and anxiety?

I am opposed to the use of dangerous drugs to treat depression and anxiety in an otherwise healthy person. There are cases when drugs are necessary, and I trust that a capable psychiatrist knows when to prescribe such medications. However, it is as simple as walking into any doctor's office to have an anti-depressant drug prescribed. Anyone can search the internet for the list of symptoms needed to get a prescription, then walk into his doctor's office and simply repeat what he read. Just as a chiropractor once told me that he would be out of business if people just stretched for 10 minutes a day, a medical doctor relies on people's ignorance to what I've written about to keep his waiting room filled with people who just can't seem to be happy. Depression and anxiety, when not caused by an underlying medical reason, can be healed by stripping the layers of garbage in people's minds that create the smoke of virtual reality between their true selves and the matrix.

13. **You said that you are giving all of the proceeds from this book to a children's charity. Why would you do that?**

When I was very young, I remember a freezing cold Christmas night when our oil burner (heating system) in our house suddenly stopped working. My mother practically begged my father to take me and my two brothers into his house, just two miles away – so we would be able to sleep in a warm house on Christmas Eve. He refused. My brothers and I slept close to a wood burning stove as my mother stayed up all night,

Michael Evans

burning pieces of newspaper to keep us warm. The next morning, on Christmas, the pipes in our house had burst because they were frozen. Water began to flood the house. My mother called several companies to ask for immediate assistance; the only catch was that she had no money to pay anyone. Then she contacted someone who was ready to help. He showed up on Christmas morning with his son (a teenager) and they worked for hours, fixing the pipes and using buckets to get the water out of our house. When it came time to pay, they refused to accept payment (that we obviously didn't have). To make things worse, only hours later, our pipes burst in another location and the father and son came back and worked for hours for free. They gave up their holiday at home together to help a poor family and a single mother who had clearly run out of options. That father and son taught

The Real Matrix

me a lesson that I will never forget. I go out of my way to live up to what those unknown men did for me and my family that day. So, it is in their names (if only I knew their names) that I pay it forward to anyone in need, especially women and children.

Chapter 1

The Real Matrix

For the next 60 minutes, I'd like you to willingly suspend your skepticism of new ideas. However, what I am about to tell you is in no way a new idea. What if I told you that you're a liar? What if I told you that your family, your closest friends and *even you* have no idea who you really are? More than that, what if I told you that you don't know *what* you are? If you did, everything that you've ever wanted for yourself in your life would be at your disposal.

Michael Evans

What is the Matrix?

If you're like most people, you have the misconception that you are the image you see in the mirror. You may also believe that it's possible for someone to hurt your feelings, that guilt and worry are normal emotions and that your past is indicative of what your future will be. Are you the kind of person that holds a grudge? If so, sit back and listen, because it's all about to change.

Before you can understand what you are, you need to take a close look at what you've been taught. Most of us grow up to believe that we are 'what we do' and we are 'what we have.' Our modern society has taught us that we are smart or we are stupid – based on our school grades. The same society has taught us that winning is the most important part of a game, that

The Real Matrix

the more possessions you have – the more successful you are. Modern medicine has taught us that we need health insurance and drugs in order to survive. Our education system teaches us that children have learning problems and need to repeat the first grade when that child is not on the same learning level as the rest of the children in his class. Religion has taught us that we need to beg for forgiveness and that we are only worthy of love if we profess our loyalty to our god. Our own experience has taught us that everyone is out to get us; to trust nobody and that there's never enough money in our accounts. Our media teaches us that rainy weather is a bad thing, to brace for the rising price of oil, and only days later, that the *falling* price of oil is bad thing. Our popular magazines teach us that a particular actress is a rising star, and then 6 months later they tell us that the same

Michael Evans

rising star is a drug addict and a disgrace to her fans, and then 6 months later they portray her as a saint and a successful actress. Our social media has taught us that it's ok to gossip about other people and that by posting carefully selected selfie photos; we can fool people into believing we are happy, rich, beautiful and content in life. With all of these misconceptions and lies, how could anyone expect to feel good about anything and more importantly – *themselves?*

Many years ago, I sat in a lecture by Wayne Dyer and he told this story. He said, "A little girl sits in her classroom while her teacher stands at the front of the class. The teacher is holding an orange in his hand and he asks the girl, "If I squeeze this orange, what will come out?" The little girl replies, "Orange juice… *that was easy!*" The teacher agrees and asks, "*Why* does

The Real Matrix

orange juice come out when I squeeze this orange?" and the girl quickly replies, "Because that's what is inside." The little girl is correct. *Now* let's expand that example and I ask you, "What happens when someone squeezes you?" What comes out of you is what you're holding inside; among other things, it could be fear, anger, jealousy or sadness. We see this every day when people react to what we say or do. We see this in ourselves and until now, we haven't taken the time to figure out exactly why. Let's examine this…

A man is 30 years old. He's a college graduate; he's married with children and earns a comfortable living as an attorney. He drives nice cars, wears nice clothing and seems to have his life together. People are envious of his life. In front of other people, he's an outgoing guy and he seems happy. But on the

Michael Evans

inside, he is constantly battling depression, thoughts of suicide, constant stress headaches and his mind races all day and night – preventing him from sleeping well. So, like many others, he stops at the local pub for a few drinks on his way home to unwind. He suddenly feels better. For a short while, his headache is gone, his worries seem to disappear and his mind slows down. When he gets home, the numbing effects of the alcohol subside and his headache reappears and his worries begin to dominate his thoughts once again. The pain is getting so bad that he goes to his doctor. His doctor listens carefully to his symptoms and tells him, "you are suffering from depression; here's some pills that will make you feel better again." The man takes the pills and they seem to slow his racing mind down, but they also make him tired and they completely slow down his sex drive. So he visits his doctor and his doctor carefully listens once again to his symptoms. His doctor tells him, "you are suffering from erectile dysfunction; here are some pills." So he takes the new pills and they artificially cure his erectile dysfunction. Only problem with *that* is, while he can now *physically* have sex, *emotionally* he is still drained and not interested. As time goes by, he becomes addicted to the pills that slow his mind down and that leads him to rely on the pills that artificially cure his erectile dysfunction. This only puts the man into a deeper depression. So deep, that his wife and kids are too much for him to handle. He is easily set off into fits of rage when he can't find his car keys, and every little thing makes him angry. How did this man's life get so out of control? The answer is simple, but getting you to believe it may not be. The answer is - he is causing all of his suffering. He

Michael Evans

is causing his mind to race, his muscles to be tense - leading to a headache and his depression is a result of him thinking the same self-defeating thoughts over and over again – and then believing them. Let's take journey into this man's day.

Its 6:00am when an obnoxious, screeching alarm clock sounds to awaken him. He jumps up, abruptly, out of a sound sleep – putting his body into an immediate fight or flight mode. His heart pounds for a few minutes until his body readjusts to realize there is no threat to his life. Before he gets out of bed, he reaches over for his phone. As he turns it on, he dreads each and every missed email and text that have been waiting all night to bring certain anxiety to his morning. He sifts through emailed complaints from clients, impossible deadlines from his boss and

The Real Matrix

spam emails from drug companies trying to sell him weight loss products, featuring a musclebound, photo-shopped image of a man he wishes to be once again. He opens his social media page, only to see that his digital friends are in an argument over an event that someone posted from the news. He reads as the comments start off with friendly opinions and commentary, and without missing a beat, someone pours their poison into the comment thread, thereby infecting the conversation with hatred and low energy. He reads as civilized men and women curse each other and as people take sides. Soon the comment thread has nothing to do with the original story. Just when he's had enough of the non-sense on his phone, he turns on the news. He's watches as the news station announces with carefully designed music and graphic work that a reporter is on "Storm Watch!" He listens to the

Michael Evans

reporter who is standing in the street as plows pass by as she grabs a pedestrian so they can tell the people at home to "stay indoors, it's dangerous outside, roads are slippery" and so on… The news switches back to the studio reporters, sitting at their desks, as they describe how everyone is *"Bracing* for the increase in oil prices!" and that people are *"Struggling* to heat their homes this winter." The next story is one that he has seen for the last 15 years - 10 times a day; "Terrorism is on the rise!" or "30 dead from suicide bomber!" Just when he's about to get out of bed, his favorite traffic girl lets him know just how bad the traffic is today. Carefully placed red marks along a picture of the highway shows just how bad his commute is about to be. He walks downstairs and reaches into the refrigerator and pours a tall glass of orange juice. He drinks it down, spiking his blood sugar level as he does every morning. Couple

The Real Matrix

that spike in blood sugar with the stressful morning he has just lived through and the traffic jam he is about to endure, and that leads his body to release a stress hormone called cortisol – affecting his attention span, short term memory and mood stability. He gets into his car and heads to the city. He is immediately met with bumper to bumper traffic when he enters the highway. Horns are honking; people are yelling at each other to, "Move!" He drowns out the sounds of this madness with is car radio. He listens to his favorite talk show personalities as they gossip about what happened on the latest reality show that aired last night. In between tirades by the talk show hosts, he is forced to listen to an obnoxious commercial by a local car dealership as they repeatedly shout out to the listeners that they are all "Approved! Good credit, bad credit, you're approved!" Then he hears at the

Michael Evans

end of that ridiculous commercial, a voice, talking faster than any human being he has ever heard, as this voice *disclaims* everything he just listened to in the commercial. When the man finally gets to his office, he sighs and says, without any regard for this autopilot conversation piece, "Good morning!" to his secretary. And so his day begins… *He is living in the Matrix.*

I'll leave the rest of this day to your imagination, but a point I'd like to make is that most people who experience days like this one, re-live them day after day. If a person lives to be 75 years old, that's about 27,000 days. When you choose to live the same day over and over, you are living one day – in this case in hell – 27,000 times. I'm here to tell you that you can choose to live 27,000 days – each day different from the next. It's your choice. Because you've lived like

The Real Matrix

this in the past, doesn't mean that you have to live like this ever again. You can change this right now. As a matter of fact, the only time to make a change is now. The future hasn't happened yet, so making a plan to change in the future is you actually worrying about something that hasn't happened yet and may *never* happen. Think about the future as a debt you may never owe. Why pay interest today on a debt that you may never owe? That interest is the suffering you experience when your emotional body believes a story that *you* are telling *yourself in your mind*. If it's about a future event, then you are surely imagining the event, creating the story or future debt you may never owe, then paying the price for it – right here and now. If you're worrying or feeling guilty about something that has already occurred, then you are paying interest on a debt that you have already paid. Imagine paying off

Michael Evans

a car loan, and then paying more interest for the rest of your life on that car loan that you've *already paid*. The past is over and done with and it has no timeline. Our society teaches us that we must feel guilty when we say or do something that is outside of societal rules. Rules that were created by the *very people* in that Matrix I descried a few moments ago. People living in hell are making the rules and we wonder why our lives are filled with negativity. Wayne Dyer put it this way, "The past is like the wake of the boat. It's not the wake that drives the boat." To that I would add, "The past is yesterday's garbage. Why in the *world* would I reach into yesterday's garbage to prepare today's meal?" Feeling guilty about a past event, worrying about a future event – especially one that may never happen – is you living your life in the Matrix; a place

The Real Matrix

where you are immobilized from doing exactly what it is that you want and have always wanted.

Why are so many people living in the matrix? I believe that most people do not know that they are creating their own reality. In their minds, life is happening *to* them, rather than *for* them. We learn this and most of our beliefs as children from the adults in our lives. As children, we are forced to endure long days in a school system that teaches us that we are one of the labels that the system places on us, such as average, above average, advanced, athletic or not athletic, popular or not popular and these labels follow us as we believe them and become exactly what others have decided about us – without ever knowing us. Children are being taught to memorize battle dates, other people's formulas and knowledge and

Michael Evans

then they are tested on this non-sense. Then, they are labeled with a test score. Children are forced into sports that they have little to no interest in playing, many times as their parents compete for watercooler stories of "My child's team won the championship, or my child's team was cheated." Many times there are children who are not playing at the same level as the other children on the team and the parents put pressure on their child to compete. They even punish their child for missing a shot, striking out or not being fast enough on the field. Did it ever occur to that parent that their child isn't interested in that or any sport? A child may dislike a particular sport that we, as parents, force him to play. His lack of interest leads to poor performance. But that child may be a brilliant musician or a creative writer, and he's being judged, labeled and forced to suffer in order to fit into

The Real Matrix

this competitive society he was raised in. If that child is out of his element, and you judge or label him, it's like judging a fish on its ability to climb a tree. Try having a swimming contest with him instead. All of this push-pull stress becomes part of a person's life at a very young age. As Don Miguel Ruiz puts it, "We live in this society, we grew up in this society and we learn to be like everyone else, playing non-sense all the time."

Chapter 2

How do we get out of the Matrix?

"The ancestor to every action is a thought"

-Ralph Waldo Emerson

Take a look at anything in front of you right now. For me, it's my laptop computer. How did my laptop computer become what it is? The answer is, with a thought. Someone, somewhere envisioned this laptop computer at some point in time, then he synchronized his energy in his body and his mind in a method called unity consciousness. Without that original

Michael Evans

thought, this laptop wouldn't be possible. This leads us to understand that what we think about, what we place our attention on, is what expands into our reality. When our mind is dominated with negative thoughts, conversations and judgements, we create the very hell we experience in our reality – that hell is what I call the matrix. The same way we can create the hell we have been living in, we can create heaven on earth. Yes, I said heaven. You don't have to wait to die in order to experience the conscious level that is heaven. You are connected to an energy that is greater than all of us, that which you came from, will return to and have access to right now. Some people choose to call it God. It doesn't matter what you call it. The very God you have been seeking all of your life is within you, not outside of you. I am not suggesting that you change your beliefs about religion, I am not

The Real Matrix

asking you to believe what I am telling you – I am asking you to remember. Remember what you have forgotten. As a fetus, you had everything you needed to survive. You had a knowing that you were perfect just as you were. There were no judgements and no gossip, no lies that you believed about yourself that became limits you set and then followed for the rest of your life. You didn't possess the properly credentialed medical doctor certificate, yet your heart knew exactly how to pump blood and nutrients into your body; your kidneys knew exactly how to filter toxins and this collective consciousness from which you came from was all you knew. For the first few years of your life, you trusted in this consciousness and your own intuition to guide you to see the truth. When you wanted to walk, you made the decision to get up and walk. When you fell, you didn't judge yourself;

Michael Evans

you got back up and soon you were walking. When other children did something that upset you - you cried. Then moments later, you let it go and you played again; never to think about that incident again. But somewhere along the way, you learned that the adults in your life have forgotten about this playful spirit. They took on serious faces, serious jobs, fancy titles and they began to demand respect. They used punishment and reward to domesticate you to become an acceptable human being in their eyes. Their biggest mistake was interfering in your life. Instead of practicing non-interference, they chose to hand you your beliefs about everything. Your religion, your self-worth, your social status and your limits were all handed to you by the adults in your life; and you continued to let this take you further out of the

The Real Matrix

collective consciousness you once lived in and has landed you directly in the matrix.

I want you to forgive your parents right now. I want you to forgive anyone who poured their beliefs into your mind. I want you to try to remember the worst memory you have as a child. For me, it was watching my father brutally assault my mother when I was just 3 years old. That was a scene I watched and internalized as a child many times. That, among other reasons, led me to fear my father and to hold a secret, long-lived hatred of him up until a few years ago. You see, I realized that I was hurting myself by not releasing my father's actions from my mind, from my heart. Holding onto that hatred and fear was like me holding in a hot mouthful of battery acid, just waiting to spit it back at him at some point. I realized that by

Michael Evans

holding this in, I was damaging my life, my internal organs, my sleep and my peace. So, I forgave him. I said it out loud, "Dad, I forgive you. I release you from my life and all that I have been holding inside of me, I release all of it. From now on, I send you love." And just like that, a weight that I had carried around on my back in the form of tension, headaches and suffering was released forever. I realized that forgiveness was about me and not my father. What he has chosen to do in his life was his karma, how I decided to deal with it was mine. I extend this opportunity to you. Anyone who has hurt you in the past – forgive them right now. You don't have to speak with them or even let them know that you forgive them, but you have to release them from your life, from your back, your heart and your dreams if you are to move forward. Leave their misdeeds and their hurtful words in your wake and start driving the boat – right now. Your point of power over them - is *now*. Remember, the past is over and the future doesn't yet exist, so you have no power in either of those dimensions that you keep replaying in your mind; it's like chasing ghosts. A ghost has no choice but to live in the past, but you are very much alive in this moment, the only moment that has ever mattered. Let's take the journey together, right now, to release all of the lies, the ghosts and negative layers that we have attracted in our lives that have created the smoke screen between the matrix and our true selves - our authentic selves, the happy wandering spirits we once were. Let's get out of this feeling of constant striving and never arriving to where we want to be in life. Maybe you are contemplating a career change or maybe you there's a business you have always wanted to open, a person you've always

Michael Evans

wanted to meet. There's a method to achieving all of those things and it starts with your mind. Remember, what you place your attention on is what expands in your life. Here's how I changed my life of growing up poor, having the worst grades in my high school, a reputation of being a disturbing element in my classes, having brushes with the law and living my first few months in college, planning my own suicide. I decided that rock bottom was not the place for me and if suicide was the alternative, I had nothing to lose by moving in the direction of my dreams – no matter what anyone thought of my pipe dream. The good news… It all came true; all of it. With all of the love in my heart, I will share with you exactly how to go from living in the matrix the way I did - as a troubled teen - to the CEO of an international company, a writer and a person who lives each and every one of those 27,000

The Real Matrix

days in nothing but love. I can tell you that you are love, you are God, you are light and everything else is just a dream. Here's the secret door to your exit out of the real matrix.

CHAPTER 3

The Law of Attraction and the Dream of Your Life

"All that will ever be is what is happening here." These are words from Jim Carey in a speech he made some years ago. What he was referring to is that most of what happens in our lives is actually happening in our mind. Your mind dreams, which is its main function. You are dreaming when you are awake and you dream when you are asleep. All day and night, there's a movie playing in your head. It's a movie and you are the writer, director and the star of that movie. In your movie, you assign roles to every person you know and encounter - and those people play their

Michael Evans

part. In your movie, they look, act and sound a certain way, based upon your perception. If I were to walk into a dark Movie Theater that was completely empty, except for my wife sitting in the front row – then sit next to her, I could observe her dream (movie) from her perspective. In that dream, I would see people that resemble me, resemble her and people we know. They would look completely different in her dream than in mine. For example, I might be skinny in her movie and speak with a very loud, obnoxious voice in her dream. In my dream, I speak quietly and I'm not skinny. It's all perception. The reason for explaining this theory is because most of life is happening in your mind. Getting back to Jim Carey's quote, "All that will ever be is what is happening here." He's stating that nothing happens until something moves. You are creating the reality that you are living in. The good

The Real Matrix

news is that using my movie theater example above, your reality is being created by you - for you. Everyone else is creating their reality as well. The Toltec call this the dream of the planet; the cumulative dream of all people.

If we are creating our own dream, how do we control it? The answer is – with your thoughts. The ancestor to every action is a thought. What you place your attention on is what expands or manifests in life. It's not simply the thought that makes this possible, but the feeling. Your emotional body reacts to your thoughts and the results vary. You can, however, manifest exactly what you do not want, by placing your attention on something you don't want. Unfortunately, it works both ways. Many people unknowingly choose to put their attention on what they do not want, by way of

Michael Evans

guilt and worry; guilt over something that is over and done with and worry about what is going to happen. The only place for those futile emotions to exist is in your own personal dream and you can choose to let them go at any time. By placing your attention (thoughts) on something you do want in life, you are creating the catalyst to manifest it.

There's a voice in your head. It has been there since you were born. That voice is constantly talking to you, but is it you? Don Miguel Ruiz calls it the "Voice of Knowledge." Whatever you choose to call it, let's examine what it is telling you and how you are reacting to it. That voice is not known for telling the truth. It tells you things and your emotional body reacts to what it says. When your emotional body reacts, you align yourself, vibrationally, with what you believe about yourself. Don Miguel Ruiz puts it this way, "The only way to change your story is to change what you believe about yourself. If you clean up the lies you believe about yourself, the lies you believe about everybody else will change. Every time you change the main character of your story, the whole story changes to adapt to the new main character."

How can you use this information moving forward? Start with an old saying that is actually backward. People say, "I'll believe it when I see it." The truth is you'll see it *when you believe it.* You must align yourself with what you want in life. You must see yourself as having what you want and you must feel the way you would if it were already true – you must believe it. My friend is a professional singer. She has a beautiful voice. She sings a few nights a week in

Michael Evans

different venues and makes a nice living doing what she loves. She is very talented and since the day I met her, she had been waiting to "be a singer." This was very confusing to me. I was speaking with her one day and I had to say it over and over again until it finally clicked. "You are already there. You are a star" (and a great one). I told her, just the way I am telling you, that money, cars and private jets are merely a side effect of your success – not the success itself. If you are doing what you love, doing your best, with a pure heart – let go of the result. The universe will align itself to synchronize with your dream. This is how some of the most successful people in history got to where they are. It's called the law of attraction.

You'll see above, that I said "pure of heart." What does that actually mean? It means when you do

The Real Matrix

something, stop asking, "What's in it for me?" When I stopped asking, "what's in it for Michael Evans", everything I ever wanted just showed up. This includes my very best friends I have today, most of which are unlikely matches to the outside person looking in. But that's ok, because that is their dream -their reality.

Did you know that before Jim Carey "made it" in show business, he understood all of these concepts I am sharing now? He even wrote himself a $10 Million dollar check for acting services rendered and kept it in his wallet for a few years while he waited for that money to manifest. He visualized his success and aligned himself with his desire and simply let go of the resistance that he himself created when he was younger. Many years ago, I did the same thing. I didn't write a check, but I became the CEO of a large

Michael Evans

international security firm (one that hadn't come to fruition yet) and I aligned myself with my desire to be who I am right now. The one thing I did not do is worry about what others thought of my choices. If you've read any of my books, you'll recognize the Gilbert K. Chesterson quote, "I owe my success to having listened respectfully to the very best advice and then going away and doing the exact opposite." The world is full of people who are dreaming the dream of hell. The very thought of your success in their dream puts them deeper into hell. Look for the people who inspire you and accept your dream as your own - this will eliminate much of the outside resistance. The rest is up to you. I'll end this chapter with my own quote, "This whole inherited idea called life is nothing more than a dream - *but you believe it.*"

Chapter 4

There's Nothing to Worry About

There's nothing to worry about. That's a pretty big claim for me to make to someone who is suffering right now. What if I told you that suffering is a choice, and so many people unknowingly choose it? Not to be confused with pain. Although people use pain and suffering in the same sentence as if it goes together automatically, like peanut butter and jelly. Pain is a result of physical injury, while suffering is related to your mind telling you something that leads your emotional body to react and suffering is the result.

Michael Evans

In the Death of Ivan Ilych, written by Leo Tolstoy in the 1800's, a famous quote emerged which was, "What if my whole life was wrong?" This was contemplated by the book's main character as he lay, dying. I propose that same question to you. What if your whole life is wrong? How would you know? Let's examine a few areas of all of our lives and see where we might be a little off or completely out of vibration with our purpose here on our breathtakingly short journey as humans.

I started this chapter, stating that there's nothing to worry about. There's a story I once read about a man named Jesse, similar to Ivan Ilych, who was on his death bed as he contemplated all of suffering that he endured in his life. As he defended his point of view about the suffering, he realized that most of the things

The Real Matrix

he was defending never really happened to him. He suffered because he was conditioned to suffer by the people who taught him how to be a human such as his parents, teachers, siblings, bosses and friends. He was taught that there's not enough money in the world, that the more money and possessions you accumulate- the better, and that jealousy and gossip are normal. He was shown by his parents who argued that forgiveness is a sign of weakness. With all of those opinions about how he should live, he quietly took on his role as a worker somewhere and he envied people who drove nice cars and lived in big houses. He could never make enough money and his boss was always riding him to work harder. With all of this suffering, his point of view got so jaded, that he hated everyone, including himself. In his mind, everyone was out to get him and he was going to get the best of everyone

Michael Evans

first in this game that he played against himself in his mind. He couldn't be happy for anyone because he wasn't happy with himself. If his friend got a new car, it was like a dagger being pushed into his heart. Jesse felt pain as if the car had anything to do with him. In his mind, his friend getting a car was something that was happening to him and he suffered as a result. Let's examine this as it is relevant in our society.

Person A and Person B are married (let's call them AB). Person C lives next door to AB. If Persons AB live a lifestyle of relaxing in the pool together every day and Person C lives a life of 12 hour work days in the blistering sun at a job he doesn't like – then Person C has a choice. He can make a change or stay in his life that he doesn't like. Now Person AB buys himself a new car. Person C has another choice – be happy for them, be indifferent and have no thoughts or opinion about their car or he can choose to suffer because of it. Memetic programming by others (like Jesse) teaches Person C to be jealous, to gossip and to ultimately suffer – when nothing happened. The point is, Person C, acting on autopilot and from his training – chose to suffer. Now multiply that by all of the new cars, houses, vacations that Person AB enjoy, and Person C's suffering is never ending. His point of view is fear based and he can't possibly be happy for anyone because he cannot give what he doesn't have – his own happiness.

I often ask my children a question when I see them torturing themselves over the achievements of others. I ask, "Is there a wolf about to eat you?" The answer is always, "of course not!" To which I reply, "Then

Michael Evans

stop tricking your body into believing it." The body is programmed with a fight or flight response mechanism. Long before humans had houses, guns and cities, we lived amongst animals that were higher on the food chain than we were. Take wolves for example; if a human were to awaken to the sound of a wolf with its mouth-watering and teeth glistening a few thousand years ago, our bodies would go into fight or flight (or freeze) mode. That stressful response was designed to keep us alive. Today, however, humans have learned to use this mechanism against ourselves. We create the wolves in our mind by our perception of events outside of us, which in turn creates the physiological reaction on our emotional bodies. We call it stress and we accept that stress is a part of life; then comes the need for medication, alcohol and drugs to numb

The Real Matrix

ourselves from the wolves that we have and continue to create in our minds.

About 20 years ago, in my first police academy, I sat on the first day, nervously waiting for the academy to start. There were about 30 trainees in the classroom. Suddenly, the door bursts open and a masked man runs into the room, yells for everyone to sit down and be quiet. He then grabbed some papers from the desk and ran out. One minute later, an academy instructor entered the room and handed us all a sheet of paper and a pen. Our assignment was to accurately describe exactly what had just occurred. I remember thinking to myself, I'm going to ace this assignment. I went on to write about the suspect who broke into the school, wearing a mask, and committed larceny and then fled. I described his clothing, his height, weight and his voice, accent, etc… When the instructor read all of our narratives out loud, it occurred to me, that there were 30 different stories being told and some of them were so far off from the story I wrote. Some trainees saw the masked man as a person who is sick and wore a mask for their protection against bacteria, and other didn't even see a mask. There were some trainees that didn't see any crime being committed and others who saw an egregious criminal act. The lesson learned at that time was, as on officer interviewing witnesses, you will likely get a different story from each one. Now take that example and multiply it by the 7+ billion people on this planet – all perceiving things from their point of view. The next time someone doesn't agree with you on something, try to remember that they are seeing things from their point of view. I've written in earlier chapters that your mind is dreaming all of the time.

The Real Matrix

You are casting, writing, directing and starring in our own story in your mind. Your point of view is the camera angle from which you always see and perceive things. It is from this point of view, you have another choice; the track of love or the track of fear. In the track of fear, everything you perceive through your lens is ugly, sad and depressing. In this track, jealousy and envy dominate your point of view. In the track of love, you no longer hold on to those self-defeating ideas and thoughts. You perceive everything with love in yourself and others – always. Going back to my police academy assignment, I put myself into this law enforcement mindset, where everything looked like a crime and everyone looked like the good guy or the bad guy. I made the choice to have that mindset and my brain filled in the blanks to my story. I perceived everything as good or bad and my knowledge created

Michael Evans

the smoke in between me and the mirror of virtual reality that I was observing.

Knowledge and truth are not synonymous. They never were. You can learn a lot of other people's math formulas, content from history books and right or wrong and it's just knowledge. It's only true when you agree with it - and even then, it's only true for you. A child sits in a classroom and his teacher places a hot dog in front him. The teacher says, "This is a hot dog." The child, being 5 years old, sees this object for the first time in his life. He asks, "What is it made of?" The teacher replies, "actually, its head meat, fatty tissue, blood, liver and other parts trimmed from animals, then rolled up and cooked, but we call it a hot dog." The child asks, "Why isn't it called head meat, fatty tissue, blood, liver and other parts trimmed from animals,

The Real Matrix

then rolled up and cooked?" The teacher rolls her eyes and the child is given a poor performance evaluation because he didn't understand that the atrocity in front of him was a hot dog by majority vote of the people in the world who choose to label things. Is it really a hot dog? Is knowledge really the truth? Is the story in your mind and your perception and the labels put on things really the truth?

Marijuana is a plant. For many years, I was convinced that it was a drug because the FDA labeled it such and the law (written by humans) made this natural plant illegal. I made the choice to agree with this knowledge and as a law enforcement officer I actively pursued users and sellers of this plant and arrested them. From my point of view, I was getting the bad guys. Don't get me wrong, there were some

Michael Evans

instances (especially when people would drive under the influence) when they needed to be stopped and dealt with, but the others were merely doing what millions of other people do with alcohol – numbing themselves from the suffering caused by the emotional reaction to the story in their minds. Now as marijuana is becoming legalized more and more, we are asked to look at marijuana differently – when nothing has changed. Marijuana hasn't changed; the effects haven't changed; only the knowledge has changed. With this shift in knowledge, comes the shift in your point of view to match the majority of other people's points of view. Now you're normal to think marijuana is acceptable, whereas if you said that last year, you were looked upon cross eyed. This same theory comes up when the topic of sex is being discussed. While we are all humans with the same reproductive system, the

The Real Matrix

age at which people may legally have sex varies and the ages may surprise you. In Albania, Germany, Austria and Italy, a 14 year old male or female can legally have sex with anyone of any age when they consent to do so. Therefore, in these countries, it is socially acceptable to notice a 14 year old girl and think or say she is pretty. Now, if a man in New York were to say that out loud, he would be labeled a pedophile by his peers and if he were to act on that, he would be arrested, jailed and labeled a sex offender for the rest of his life. Humans create knowledge – then expect you to shift your point of view to accept it. They create labels and expect you to memorize them and agree with them. A hot dog is not necessarily a hot dog; marijuana is not necessarily a drug. Is everyone in these other developed and modern countries wrong?

Michael Evans

Are the people of Uruguay criminals when they smoke a joint?

I started this chapter by saying there's nothing to worry about. I'd like to change that up a little and say, "There's nothing to defend." Just like Ivan Ilych and Jesse in the examples above, life is just that, life. On your short journey on this planet, make the choice not to suffer, see things for what they really are and drop labels and for Pete's sake, know the difference between the thought of a wolf about to eat you and an actual wolf about to eat you. The first will save your life on the spot and the latter will save you from all of those terrible things that never really happened anyway.

Chapter 5

Getting Off of Autopilot

The average person is awake for 960 minutes per day. Did you know that the subconscious mind dominates 95% of your thinking throughout the day; that's 912 of 960 minutes when you're acting on autopilot? You're not deliberately thinking. If you're on autopilot, where did the information in your subconscious come from? The answer may surprise you. The information in your subconscious was programmed by the teachers in your life, mostly when you were a child. When I say teachers, I am not necessarily talking about school teachers – although they are included. Your teachers in

Michael Evans

life that supplied the information to your subconscious mind are the adults, parents, older siblings, friends, etc. As a child, beginning in the womb, you learn to be like your teachers and to accept what these teachers say and do as the truth. This information is like a download in our brain. These downloads are known as memes. Memes are ideas that are spread from one person to another. Memes form the basis of knowledge from which you perceive things. Your perception is therefore impacted by beliefs that were never yours to begin with.

Picture a 5 year old child at the beach with her parents. Mom and dad are having an intense argument about money and their bills when the little girl asks her dad to build a sand castle with her. He ignores her, so she asks again and again. He finally replies

The Real Matrix

in a loud voice, "No! Can't you see the adults are talking?" The little girl just learned a painful lesson – that she is not good enough to speak when adults are talking. This becomes a meme (an autopilot download of knowledge) that will be recalled during her lifetime in that 95% of time when she is on autopilot. At age 6 the same girl asks her parents if she can take dance lessons. Her parents tell her that she is not coordinated enough to dance and she will embarrass herself if she tries. Two more memes are downloaded for future use while on autopilot (I'm not coordinated and if I try to do something outside of my comfort zone, I will be embarrassed). This list of memes goes on and on. Most of the memes you were programmed with are not even true, but you believe them.

Michael Evans

The Toltecs referred to the subconscious dominant mind activity as a dream. If we agree with that, then we must agree that we are dreaming all of the time. Remembering the 2 examples of how memes are programmed into a child's mind for use throughout their lives, then we can clearly see that their dream is not necessarily true. Our perception of events outside of us are guided by the knowledge (memes) programmed by adults when we were children. Our reactions to those events, guided by our perception, led by our knowledge, leads to physiological responses in our emotional body. As I have explained before, the emotional body reacts with a fight or flight (stress) mechanism, which in turn sends masses of blood to the arms and legs. When that blood is distributed in this manner, the visceral organs are stripped of the blood that carries the nutrients necessary for growth

The Real Matrix

and proper function. Therefore, being in a constant state of stress, which is really a fight or flight state, will significantly impact your physical health, stunt your growth and ultimately take years off of your life.

You've all heard of the sixth sense. Some of you do not believe that there is a sixth sense. I'm here to tell you that the sixth sense is really your first sense. Earlier, I spoke about the fact that the fight or flight response draws blood from your visceral organs. You can physically feel that happening. Right now, close your eyes and picture yourself standing on the world's tallest building. Picture yourself leaning over the edge on a windy day and suddenly slipping and you begin to free fall to certain death. Notice the feeling in your body, the apparent drop in blood pressure and the tingling you get in your arms and in your

Michael Evans

belly. That is your body's fight or flight response. Now you know what it feels like and that you can bring it on by merely thinking of a stressful situation. With this awareness, you can now pay attention to your emotional body's reactions to situations. That awareness is known as intuition. With intuition, you pay close attention to your body's reactions to people, events and ideas. Intuition is your sixth sense. If you make it your first sense, you will begin to hone in on the collective intelligence that you've dismissed in the name of superstitious phenomena. Pay close attention to your intuition and let it lead you. Use your other five senses to support your intuition. When you begin to focus on this task, you begin to deliberately think – taking yourself off of autopilot and arriving right here and now.

The Real Matrix

As for the memes... The only way to change them is to dismiss your attachment to them. This is done deliberately and will take time and practice. In order to clear your mind, you must let go of the beliefs that you never really chose to believe in the first place. There's an excellent book that I recommend if you want to know and understand this process. It's called the Five Levels of Attachment, by Don Miguel Ruiz Jr.

Chapter 6

The Real Butterfly Effect

> *"Every left, every right, every pause in your breath for your entire existence has changed the world for every human being in it."*
>
> ~Michael Evans

A little league baseball player stands at bat in front of a crowd of parents and other spectators. It's the bottom of the ninth inning and the count is full, 3 balls, two strikes and the game is tied. The bases

Michael Evans

are loaded with two outs. The child pitching takes an extra 10 seconds before he throws the pitch. The batter nervously awaits the pitch. If that batter swings and misses, the game goes into extra innings and can last for several minutes to an hour. If he swings and gets a base hit, the game is over. What happens next will change the world forever. Yes, I said the "world" "forever." Let's examine this theory...

Let's assume on the same evening of this little league game, the batter won the game for his team by hitting a single. The parents gather their kids' equipment and head to their cars. Let's also assume its 5:00PM when they leave the parking lot. On their way home the batter's father stops at a red light and then proceeds at the green light at 5:02:07PM (7 seconds). Just then a driver in an oncoming vehicle decides to try to beat

The Real Matrix

the red light on his side and ends up striking the little league player's car on his dad's side – killing the dad.

Many of the evening's activities contributed to this accident. It's obvious that I will point out that the pitcher taking an extra 10 seconds to deliver the pitch contributed to the timing of the accident, which couldn't have occurred had the timing not been precisely 5:02:07PM. I will leave it to you to decide if this accident would've been possible if the child had struck out and the game would have gone into extra innings or if his dad would've stopped to say hello to another parent on his way to the car.

The fact is, the game had very little to do with the outcome that night. Although it seems on the surface that the decision made by the dad to take a certain route home and the decision of the driver to pass the

Michael Evans

red light were the ultimate cause of the accident, the truth is that we all contributed, even you.

Every left, every right, every single step you have taken, every pause, every conversation has changed the world. Think about it – the moment you met your husband or wife couldn't have happened if you hadn't lived your life precisely as you did from the moment you were born. More than that, if I hadn't lived my life exactly as I did, you may have never met your significant other – 3,000 miles away. We are all acting in concert to fulfill each other's destinies. That concert is known as the universe. Break it down. Uni (one) Verse (song). We are all singing the one song that moves the wind and makes the flowers grow. That song is in me, you, everyone and everything. Without it, your body is just water, blood and bones.

The Real Matrix

Because we are all acting in concert, it becomes clear that we are all connected. Humans have forgotten this. We feel disconnected from other people, the earth, animals and nature, when we are all of those things. On a molecular level, we are all the same atoms vibrating at different levels to orchestrate the virtual reality that we perceive.

The fact that you are alive today is no mistake. The universe is perfect, so mistakes are not real – they never were. Each person plays a vital role in the universe. What you may have perceived as a mistake, made it possible for you to be right here and now. In other chapters, I have spoken about the law of attraction. Knowing that the universe is the one song we are all singing, and understanding the law of attraction, you begin to understand that what you tell the universe is

Michael Evans

what the universe provides for you. Just the other day, a young man walked into the gym where I train. On his arm was a tattoo that read, "FTW" (f@ck the world). With that point of view, how could he ever expect to be happy, successful or at peace? You better believe that the universe says it back to him, with traffic jams, collection agents, arrests, stress, etc... How does this tie into the butterfly effect? The negative energy from the FTW guy ripples through the universe at the same speed as positive energy, thus creating the push-pull, ebb and flow of all of our realities. That only proves that the world can heal itself if we all conspire to make it happen – minus the FTW point of view. It starts with you. Do your best without expectation of outcome and then let go of the result. If we all do this, then we can confidently move in the direction of our dreams and know that we are properly setting

The Real Matrix

the stage for generations to come. When we do our best, pure of heart, following our intuition, we will know that we played our part in the universe and the butterfly effect, thereby eliminating the theory and ultimate possibility of regret from our futures. As Andy Andrews put it in his book, 'The Butterfly Effect: How Your Life Matters' "You have been created in order that you might make a difference. You have within you the power to change the world." To that I would add, "...so go confidently in the direction of your dreams, within the track of love, because everyone and everything depends on you."

Chapter 7

The Death of Your Old Self

"If the doors of perception were cleansed, everything would appear to man as it is, infinite."

~William Blake

The life you lived up until now - let's refer to it as the morning or your life, is over. The morning is over and it's time to step into the afternoon of your life. The old you… *is dead*, but let's redefine death. You are an infinite being, so you never die; at least, not

Michael Evans

in the sense that most people think. There's a story in Deepak Chopra's book, 'Life after Death, Burden of Proof' and in the storyline, while Savitri asked a monk how she could beat death to save her husband, he told her to "Stop believing in rumors." He said, "The only reason you believe that you were born is that your parents saw you emerge from the womb. They thought they witnessed the moment when you began to exist, so they spread the rumor that you had been born." Think about it for a minute; look for a picture of yourself as a child. You'll see that the child in that picture has long since existed. The body you have been occupying in your human experience will surely cease to exist one day. The good news is the energy; the collective consciousness that you are, is limitless, endless and can never die.

The Real Matrix

In the beginning of this book, I suggested that you may be a liar. You have been lying to yourself, to everyone around you all the time. I want you to take a moment and think about the roles you have been playing throughout your life; husband, wife, brother, sister, boyfriend, girlfriend, student, teacher, worker, boss, friend, enemy, coach, player, mentor, actor and so on. Now look at your social media profiles and compare that projected image that you portray to each one of the roles you play in life. You'll see that you play so many roles, but none of the roles is your true self. These are only images that you project. The images you project are different from the images people see when they receive your image, so therein creates another lie; the outside image of each one of your roles creates the avatar that nobody really knows and up until now, *neither did you*. When you look

Michael Evans

closely at this, you'll notice that nobody really knows who you are. It's time to let go of the worry of what others think about you, let go of the roles you play in your life and start living from your intuition, from your source, your heart, and let go of the need to be right. You'll see that your reputation is nothing but a made up story in your mind. Once you let go of the idea that you have a reputation, you have nothing to live up to. It's like moving to a new school district as a child – where nobody knows you. You can start over without living up to the reputation you carried around with you, your whole life.

It's time to start sending love to everyone and everything. Send love in response to hate; it's the only way to stop negative energy in its tracks. The only way for you to send love is to realize something

The Real Matrix

I mentioned in the beginning of this book. I said, "You don't know what you are" - so I will end this book with a quote from the Mastery of Love, by Don Miguel Ruiz, *"You will notice that you are not the dream, not the mind, and if you go deeper, you start noticing that you are not the soul either. Then what you find out is so incredible; you find out that what you are, is a force; a force that makes it possible for your body to live. A force that makes it possible for you whole mind to dream. Without you - without this force -your body would collapse on the floor. Without you, your whole dream just dissolves into nothing. What you really are is that force that is life. Life is not the body, it is not the mind, it is not the soul - it is a force. Through this force, a newborn baby becomes a child, a teenager, an adult, it reproduces and grows old. When life leaves the body, the body decomposes and turns to dust. You are life*

Michael Evans

passing through your body, passing through your mind, passing through your soul. You find out that you are the force that makes the flowers open and close, that makes the hummingbird fly from flower to flower. You find out that you are in every tree; you are in every animal, vegetable and rock. You are the force that moves the wind and breathes through your body. The whole universe is a living being that is moved by that force; and that is what you are. You are life."

Contact author at:

therealmatrixbook.com